LIVE BED SHOW

LIVE BED SHOW

by Arthur Smith

WARNER CHAPPELL PLAYS

LONDON

A Warner Music Group Company

LIVE BED SHOW
First published in 1995
by Warner Chappell Plays Ltd
129 Park Street, London W1Y 3FA

ISBN 0 85676 212 1

Printed by Commercial Colour Press, London E7

For Sarah Howell

LIVE BED SHOW was presented by Rupert Gavin for Incidental Theatre in association with Stoll Moss Theatres and PW Productions at the Garrick Theatre, London from 30th January, 1995, with the following cast:

CASH   Paul Merton

MARIA   Caroline Quentin

Directed by Audrey Cooke
Designed by Bethia Jane Green
Lighting designed by Christopher Toulmin
Additional music by Mark Bradley
Company stage manager: Ali Duncan

An earlier version of LIVE BED SHOW was presented by Rupert Gavin for Incidental Theatre at the Pleasance, as part of the Edinburgh Festival Fringe in 1989 and was nominated for both the Perrier *Pick of the Fringe* and the *Independent* awards, with the following cast:

CASH   Arthur Smith

MARIA   Caroline Quentin

Directed by Audrey Cooke
Stage Manager: Ali Duncan

The production subsequently appeared at the Donmar Warehouse Theatre, London in 1989 as part of the *Pick of the Fringe* season.

The following text is correct as of time of going to print on 18th January, 1995.

THE SET

A bed. Or beds.

COSTUMES

Pyjamas. Or not.

MUSIC

Bed's Too Big Without You — Police

The Runaway Train

Madame Butterfly — Puccini

In addition to the above songs as mentioned in the script, 'Boum' by Charles Trenet also featured in the original production.

In the dark we hear MARIA *have an orgasm. Lights up.* CASH *is sitting in bed reading the paper intently.* MARIA *is under the duvet.*

CASH   Did you say something?

            (MARIA *resurfaces.*)

MARIA   I think we should get up.

CASH   Eh?

MARIA   I think we should get up. We've been in bed too long, we should get up.

CASH   Shall I make a cup of tea?

MARIA   I don't want a cup of tea. I want to get up.

CASH   There's still some Sunday papers left.

MARIA   I'm sick of Sunday papers.

CASH   Surely not.

MARIA   Cash, it's Tuesday.

CASH   Is it? How do you know that then?

MARIA   Do you know how long we've been in bed together? Do you?

CASH   No.

MARIA   Nine years. We've been in bed together for nine years. Nearly nine and a half. We've been in bed for nearly a decade.

CASH   That was great sex.

MARIA   (*laughs, concedes*) Yes.

CASH   Warm.

MARIA   Warm.

CASH   Loving.

MARIA   Loving. Moist.

CASH   Moist.

MARIA   Dirty.

CASH   Dirty. Shall we do it again?

MARIA   No.

CASH   You mean you want a cup of tea?

MARIA   No.

CASH   The Sunday papers then?

MARIA   I don't fancy you, you know. I might love you a
            bit, but I don't fancy you.

CASH   How can you say that? We've been in bed
            together for nine years and in that time all we've
            done is make love, drink tea, read the papers,
            make love, drink tea, read the papers . . .

MARIA   Doesn't it strike you as odd that that's all we've
            done for nine years?

CASH   Odd?

MARIA   You haven't left the house in that time. You
            haven't eaten anything, you haven't worked . . .

CASH   It's not odd. It's not odd.

MARIA   You haven't been to the toilet for nine years,
            surely that's odd.

CASH   Yes I suppose that is, that is actually a bit odd.

MARIA   You know why, don't you? Because you're
            dreaming all this.

CASH   Shit. I can't be.

MARIA   Don't worry. It's not for long. Soon you'll be
            awake and I won't be in this bed. I'm not really
            in this bed now. Not really. I'm at home, in my
            own. Probably with someone else.

CASH   Who? Who are you in bed with? Is it Michael
            Buckett?

MARIA   I don't know, it's your dream.

CASH   Who?

MARIA   Don't worry. It's not for long.

            (*The bed starts to split apart into two single beds.*)

            (*dreamlike voice*) You're swimming towards
            wakefulness, you're nearly there.

CASH   Oh, and it started so well.

MARIA   I'm going.

CASH   Don't go. I'll lie on the wet spot.

MARIA   There is no wet spot. Goodbye.

            (*She exits. He gets out of bed, groans, sits on
            bed.*)

CASH   I'm thirty-five. Thirty-five years old. I'm not
            nineteen any more, I'm not thirty-four. I look
            forty-two, I feel fourteen, I am thirty-five. Old
            ladies come up to you in the street and say "I'm
            eighty-four y'know eighty-four". You try telling
            people "I'm thirty-five you know." They're not

interested. Thirty-five. I'm too old to break into professional football now.

I bumped into a bloke recently I hadn't seen for twenty-five years. "What are you doing these days?" I said. "Still at primary school?" Oddly he was. He was a headmaster. How can I be so old that I have a contemporary who's a headmaster? It must be so depressing when your friends become High Court judges. The headmaster wanted to share anecdotes about our respective kids. It's becoming increasingly apparent that I am not immortal. The evidence is piling up. I used to sleep in the foetal position. Now I've graduated to the coffin pose.

(*He lies down in the coffin pose.*)

MARIA   I estimate I've been in over 500 beds in my lifetime. I'm not saying I'm an old slapper who sleeps around, although in my time I've been an old slapper who sleeps around. I don't think I'm much above the national average for someone of my age. I've been in brass beds, pine beds, bunk beds, sofa beds, hotel beds, hospital beds. Once, and I'm not proud of this, I woke up in a flower bed. I've been in cots, couches, couchettes, chaise lounges, futons, hammocks.

Two years ago I slept in a very old four-poster bed. It really gave me the willies. I thought of all those former occupants stretching back a hundred and fifty years. Stretching back in the same bed as me. The bed was full of corpses.

CASH   (*he is snoring*) Ah excellent, I'm asleep. Let's get dreaming. Come on Maria. God, what's Ned Sherrin doing here? Maria, Maria. I'm waiting. Go away mother.

(*He sits up.*)

Dreams are brilliant and dreams are terrible. A dream is like a film you wrote, produced, directed

and starred in and you're the only one who sees
it. I've seen some goodies. I've walked in the
Himalayas with a woman I'd never even met, I'd
just seen a photograph of her on the outside of
Stockwell Underground Photo-Me Booth. Now
when I pass it I always give her a smile.

The most pointless dream is when you're lying
asleep dreaming that you're asleep. And the best
of course . . .

MARIA   Cash.

CASH   Ah, there you are.

         (*She kisses him. Stylised dance-type movement.*)

MARIA   I've missed you so profoundly.

         (*She hands him a trophy.*)

CASH   What's this?

MARIA   While you were away you were voted the sexiest
         man who ever lived.

CASH   Really? No problem about the double chin? I beat
         James Dean then?

MARIA   So easily.

CASH   Who was voting?

MARIA   Just me. I love you and not just because you're
         the finest lover in South London.

CASH   What can I say?

MARIA   I don't mind if you sleep with other women
         occasionally.

CASH   I may not want to.

MARIA   They will though.

CASH   That's true.

MARIA   While you were away Southend bought Romario
            and got promoted.

CASH   Splendid.

MARIA   Mott the Hoople have reformed.

CASH   Oh wonderful.

MARIA   Rupert drowned in a vat of his own vomit.

CASH   Rupert at work? (*Laughs.*)

MARIA   So many beautiful things. Mandovsa Road is no
            longer restricted parking. The Tories are gone but
            sex is still good. And you don't ever have to get
            up really early in the morning ever again.

            (*Four loud beeps of an alarm clock. Lighting
            changes.*)

            You sad middle-aged nobody. Why don't you do
            everyone a favour and take your own life?

            (*She exits.*)

CASH   Nightmares. I've smoked crack, I've been chased
            by Germans, I've had AIDS, I've become
            addicted to Irish dancing, I've slept with my Dad
            . . . I suppose there wouldn't have been a wet
            spot. Nine years of constant sex, the whole
            mattress would have been soaked.

            (*Music.* CASH *moves to table. He sits and reads
            back his letter. It is later and he is now slightly
            drunk, perhaps he knocks something over.*)

            Dear Maria. An old woman asked me to see her
            across the road yesterday. I was quite amused. I
            thought it only happened in Scout Manuals.
            When we'd crossed the road she gripped my arm

tighter and said, "My husband died last year my boy, and I can't afford the rent any more."

I've seen the newsreels on the telly. Poor, thin kids dying in the dust. There are people in jails being tortured to death; the old bloke next door to me has got a cat and emphysema. Even as I write I can hear him coughing, great chest-exploding, racking coughs. People can't get work, people are going blind and getting cancer and going mad. (*Laughs.*)

Dear, this is bit over the top.

I don't give a flying fuck about any of these people. Not any more. Because dear Maria, wank shit bollocks, woe is me, oh fuck it. Amazingly after all the time I have known you, I have fallen in love with you. I have.

(*Lights up on* MARIA *as well. She is reading the same letter.*)

CASH   }
MARIA   }   I have fallen in love with you.

(*Lights down on* CASH. *She continues reading.*)

MARIA   (*reading*) Since our return from Lanzarote, I have been moping around, pining like an adolescent lover in a Chaucer poem. I've got all the symptoms. I can't sleep, I feel jealous of people you talk to, I've lost interest in my work, every time the phone rings I hope it's you. This afternoon I went to the dry cleaners and the phone on the counter rang and it was someone ringing to ask if they washed duvets . . . What is he going on about . . . ? And I was really pissed off because I hoped it was you. I thought maybe you knew I was in the dry cleaners and you had rung to say that you loved me too.

This is how crap I have become. It's all very well, murder oppression, injustice, what about me? I'm miserable. If I thought it would help I would have pushed that old lady with the dead family under a bus.

It's an hour since I wrote that bit. I've had three joints and four glasses of wine and now I'm . . . (*She can't read the words.*) . . . really really . . . ready for bed. But before I do I'm going to walk round your house and deliver this. You're sober in the morning when you read this, I write pissed in the night, I'm sorry I love you, we must talk. (*She stops reading.*) Oh dear.

(*"Bed's Too Big Without You" by the Police is playing.* CASH *enters.*)

CASH   You'd have thought that Sting of all people could afford to buy himself a single bed. Do you think sex was better under Thatcher?

MARIA   It would have to have been under her — she'd never let you on top.

(CASH *laughs.*)

CASH   Do you know, there are millions of people who have never had sex under a Labour administration?

MARIA   You look like a man who might have done it under the Liberals.

CASH   Do I? Actually I did heavy petting under the Whigs.

I reckon unless you're unemployed you get a bigger hard-on under the Tories. Something to do with extremes, and danger. I bet the Blitz was sexy, all humping away in the blackout. Imagine having sex on Stockwell Underground station with your next door neighbour.

MARIA   It's hard not to some mornings.

CASH   But it would be exciting, wouldn't it?

MARIA   No, it wouldn't. My next door neighbour weighs nearly twenty stone.

CASH   Yes, mine's an old git with a cough. Fear of death must be a turn on. Death itself — they say you get an erection when you're hanged.

MARIA   Not if you're a woman.

CASH   I hate fancy dress parties. Especially when someone's wearing the same as me.

MARIA   Who are you supposed to be?

CASH   Wee Willy Wanky.

MARIA   Why are you wanky rather than winky?

CASH   Well I'm wanky 'cause I'm wearing pyjamas. Who are you?

MARIA   Rip Van Wankle, I suppose.

CASH   (*laughs*) No, I mean what's your name?

MARIA   Maria.

CASH   Hello Maria, people call me Cash.

MARIA   Hello Cash. Enjoying the party?

CASH   Well I'm enjoying the idea of it. I haven't been to a party like this for awhile.

MARIA   What, a fancy dress party?

CASH   Yes, and the sort of party where you don't get there 'till closing time and you drink too much Valpolicella, chunder in the garden, walk eight miles home and maybe a fight. Whatever happened to Party Sevens?

MARIA   Yes, come midnight there was always some rugby
          player trying to bash the top in with a
          screwdriver.

CASH   These days the parties I'm invited to all seem to
          take place on Sunday afternoons and there's more
          Perrier than beer. What was once the dope room
          is now the babies room.

MARIA   Haven't got any kids yourself then?

CASH   I have the same number of kids as I have ex-
          wives.

MARIA   I refuse to ask how many that is.

CASH   Well done. Would you like to see my Wigan
          Drop?

MARIA   Come again?

CASH   Do you want to go downstairs and dance?

MARIA   No.

CASH   No, nor do I.

MARIA   No one's dancing anyway.

CASH   It's pathetic. Do you know what I hate about the
          youth of today. I'm not one of them. Do young
          people have sex any more?

MARIA   Who cares?

CASH   I've got a terrible feeling they do.

          (*He stands.*)

          They say men think about sex every eight
          seconds. Who says? Is some bloke standing
          around with a stop-watch and a hard-on? Every
          eight seconds? Men think about sex far more
          often than that. I think about sex all the time.

There was a time when I wanted to have sex with pretty well every woman I met. Even my grandmother. I've heard people make jokes about how horrible it was to kiss their grandmother. I never minded, I quite liked the wrinkly, bristly feel on my cheek.

MARIA Women think about sex, but not frequently and pointlessly like men. On a train for example. I reckon that a man imagines a quick, violent squirting with the schoolgirl opposite. How tawdry. I imagine a long and subtle foreplay with the craggy looking man reading Dostoevsky. It's a long and complex relationship and in the end he is begging for me. But alas I have to get off at Birmingham New Street. Or . . . or . . . (*Laughs.*) A quick violent shag with the schoolboy opposite.

CASH For a woman the ideal man, apparently, has the face of Rob Lowe, the body of Linford Christie and the bottom of Mick Jagger. Well what a site that man would look. He'd be half black, half white and have an arse that's ten years older than the rest of his body. Michael Jackson, in fact.

MARIA I heard a man the other day say . . . (*Adopts voice of a coarse cockney fellow.*) "I say to this bird, loveliest bird you've ever seen, legs up to here, legs up to her armpits!" Call me unconventional but surely he'd prefer a woman with a torso.

(*They both stand.* CASH *has a cornflake packet between his teeth.* MARIA *takes the packet and hands it to* CASH. *He tears a strip off the packet and puts the packet on the floor between them.*)

CASH Right, that was the easy one. Your go.

(MARIA *picks the packet up with her teeth, then hands it back to* CASH.)

CASH Very good. (*Puts the packet back on the floor.*) Right, my go again.

MARIA   I'd love to but I've got to go and find my lift
            home.

CASH   Oh, right. Are you sure you don't want to come
            back to my place for a cup of cocoa? I only live
            round the corner.

MARIA   So do I. (*Pause.*) You don't change much do you?

CASH   Have we met before?

MARIA   You remember Alison Jenson?

CASH   My old flatmate Alison. Do you know her?

MARIA   You went to her sister's party in Leicester once.

CASH   Yes, that's right, so I did. Oh was that you in the
            garden? Oh God, how embarrassing. I'm sorry.

MARIA   I obviously made a big impression on you.

CASH   I'm sorry.

MARIA   You certainly made an impression on the garden.

CASH   I'm not like that any more.

MARIA   No? What if I suggested a quick lap of the garden
            now?

CASH   There's no garden here.

MARIA   I must go. Call me at work if you like. (*Exits.*)

CASH   God, fancy meeting someone and forgetting
            you've slept with them. It's not good is it? I felt
            awful, but not so awful that I didn't ring her up. I
            invited her to the National Film Theatre, where
            there was a Basil Brush retrospective. Boom
            Boom. Happily she said no and we went to the
            pub. I love pubs. Big, beery rooms with carpets.
            Apart from asking me if owned a garden she

didn't mention our previous encounter and we bantered gaily. I had resolved not to make a pass at her, but I got pissed and resolved to make a pass at her.

(MARIA *is sitting on the sofa.*)

CASH   I do like cocoa.

MARIA   I don't.

CASH   If I had a perfect day, it would certainly involve cocoa.

MARIA   I think I should tell you something. I'm celibate. (*Turns to audience.*) I really enjoy saying that to men. They always look surprised at first . . . then they look hurt, like a little boy who's had his Lego taken away, or else defiant as if to say "I didn't want to shag you anyway". Or there's a glimmer of challenge in their eyes. "You wouldn't want to be celibate if you saw my nob, love". I wondered how Cash would react.

CASH   Oh, well done.

It was if she'd taken my Lego away. Of course, "Do you want a cup of cocoa" was only the surface text. The subtext, the real text was "I fancy you. I want to go to bed with you. Perhaps that will be nice and perhaps we'll like each other too and form some kind of relationship. Maybe it will become monogamous and long term and love, maybe we'll have children and die together in each other's arms at the age of 142." But when she said that, there was no subtext. The subtext was gone.

(*Pause.*)

When you first go out on a date, if you're a man, you wonder if you are going to get lucky. The annoying thing is that the woman knows already.

MARIA   Not always. I used to set out on what I really
         expected to be a hot date with my toothbrush
         packed, condom, sexy underwear, the lot — but
         after half an hour with the bloke . . .

CASH   Out through the toilet window.

MARIA   If there was one. Sometimes I just went ahead
         with the whole thing because it was harder not to.
         Terrible really.

CASH   So you've slept with people you don't like?

MARIA   Haven't you?

CASH   I suppose so, but I've never knowingly slept with
         a Tory. No, that's a lie. I once had a one night
         stand with Lady Olga Maitland.

MARIA   (*laughs*) One night stand. Sounds so out of date.
         Like Party Sevens or discotheques.

CASH   One night stands. They were so glamorous,
         weren't they? For one night only, Cash and his
         famous nob jive. I'd come home on the tube on
         Sunday morning and see a girl in a party frock
         and tired make-up and I knew what she'd been
         doing. The same as me.

MARIA   The difference being that she was embarrassed
         and you were smug.

CASH   Rueful, more rueful.

MARIA   I hated all those bits leading up to the moment.
         What a palaver.

CASH   Yes. "Listen I wear contact lenses, I'll just take
         them out."

MARIA   "Fine. Where's the bathroom?"

CASH   "Through there. I'll bring you tea in the
         morning."

MARIA	"I need to be up by eight."
CASH	"Don't worry. I'll put the alarm clock on."
MARIA	"We're near a tube, aren't we?"
CASH	"By the way, mine's the blue toothbrush or did you bring one?"
MARIA	And the whole rigmarole often preceded by the big lie, "shall we just . . .
CASH MARIA }	. . . sleep together." . . . sleep together."
CASH	There have been mutually agreeable one night stands.
MARIA	I wouldn't know.
CASH	You've had one to my knowledge. More a ten second stand really.
MARIA	I suppose I have had them but they only become one night stands the next morning when I realised I could only stand them for one night.
CASH	Or vice-versa. Do you want to go?
MARIA	Do you want me to?
CASH	No.
MARIA	Then I won't.
CASH	I think I'm talking to you differently than if I was trying to get you into bed.
MARIA	Why? What would you be saying?
CASH	Don't know. I used to claim that I could make up a fantasy that would turn women on. They'd say "I bet you can't", and off you go. (*Pause.*) Do you

	want to try it? (*She looks doubtful.*) It's not a ploy. A fantasy for you and me.
MARIA	Go on then.
CASH	It's a hot sticky simmering summer, you're living on the first floor of a block of flats, quite a classy block of flats, you've a balcony on which you stand in the mornings in a silk dressing gown sipping Camomile tea. One morning as you stand there you look down . . .
MARIA	You've done this before haven't you?
CASH	Twice. Three times. It never turns out the same.
MARIA	Go one then, what am I looking down on?
CASH	Four burly workmen.
MARIA	I thought so. And it's hot so they've no shirts on, they look like Chippendales, one of them has a tattoo . . .
CASH	That's where you're wrong. It's not like that at all. Only three of them have their tops off. And of those, one has a beer gut, one is a hunchback. One has a not bad body. He's trim but has a bit of a tyre . . .
MARIA	Bit like you in fact.
CASH	You think I've got a bit of a belly?
MARIA	Shut up. Go on.
CASH	See? The first day you see the workmen, you're walking past them on the way to work, and they whistle at you and make sexist remarks. Wotcha darling! And then they do that whistle (*He tries.*) I can't do it.
MARIA	I get the idea.

CASH	Apart from one. The only one wearing a top. He smiles shyly at you, a smile of apology at his leering friends.
MARIA	So a bit of a tyre was a red herring.
CASH	Yes, and Beer Gut.
MARIA	I've grown rather fond of Hunchback.
CASH	You don't fancy him though, do you?
MARIA	Tell me about Steve.
CASH	Steve?
MARIA	The one who flashed me the smile.
CASH	Steve. Alright, Steve. Steve has beautiful white teeth, a suntan. In his faded blue jeans a small pert bum. He has an ear ring?
MARIA	Yes.
CASH	Brown eyes.
MARIA	One of them just slightly askew.
CASH	Why?
MARIA	I don't want him too perfect.
CASH	Beer Gut is game if you like.
MARIA	Of course.
CASH	You go to work, forget him and his muscular tanned torso, but when you see him again your heart gives an unexpected leap and you find yourself smiling at him. For a tiny second your eyes meet, well, as well as they can meet given his squint but he looks at you momentarily with such intensity that you feel naked before him. Then he turns and carries on digging.

MARIA   Send him up now, I'm ready.

CASH   There's no rush is there? You're celibate.

MARIA   Not in the fantasy.

CASH   As you unlock the front door of your flat you
             notice he is behind you. "Sorry", he says, "I
             didn't mean to frighten you . . ."

MARIA   He speaks.

CASH   "We need some water for our tea." He holds out a
             plastic bottle. He has beautiful clear skin, and
             smells manly.

MARIA   Sweaty.

CASH   Yes.

MARIA   Good.

CASH   You run to the kitchen. Your heart is pumping.
             You return with the bottle and offer it but he is
             staring at you. He knocks the bottle aside and
             takes you in his arms . . .

MARIA   We dance in a circle holding each other. I have
             one hand in the small of his back, beneath his T-
             shirt, the tips of my fingers pressing his spine.
             My other hand is running through his hair. His
             hand is gently massaging my scalp, we stare at
             each other through closed eyes. I know within the
             next ten seconds we are going to be locked in a
             deep french kiss and that I will be unbuttoning
             his jeans and —

             (*She suddenly stops. There is a moment between
             them.*)

CASH   Better go home.

             (*Music as the scene changes.*)

MARIA   We agreed to see a play together in a room above a pub the following week. It was called "Flowers in the Sink" and was exceedingly arty. It was also exceedingly boring.

CASH   This country is shit. The food is shit, the Government is shit, the weather is shit, the transport system is shit, education is shit, the health service is shit, the music is shit, my job is shit, TV is shit, death is shit, I am shit.

MARIA   And now the shipping forecast.

CASH   Well it is. And you're shit too. Name me one thing that isn't shit.

MARIA   Our friendship.

CASH   How wet. Do you remember that play we went to see on our second date?

MARIA   Oh God yeah.

CASH   What was it called?

MARIA   Er . . .

CASH   "Lupins in the Toilet", or something.

MARIA   Flowers . . . Flowers in the . . . Flowers in the something.

CASH   Yes.

MARIA   Now that was shit.

CASH   Oh I don't know.

MARIA   Oh come on. It was the most tedious one hour twenty-two minutes I've ever endured.

CASH   It was a bit boring, I'll grant you.

MARIA   A bit boring. I'd rather spend a week in Solihull with Richard and Judy.

CASH   Just because it was boring doesn't mean it wasn't good. I mean, look at Joyce's Ulysses, fantastically dull.

MARIA   Yes, the first three pages certainly were.

CASH   We all get bored so easily. I bet there was no boredom in the nineteenth century. They were all too busy being repressed and writing novels and dying of consumption.

MARIA   What's the matter with you?

CASH   Where shall I go on holiday?

MARIA   When are you going?

CASH   In a month or so.

MARIA   Who are you going with?

CASH   Dunno now. No one.

MARIA   Who were you going with?

CASH   Oh, Richard and Judy. No, I was going with Jenny, but she decided to stay faithful to the married man she's going out with.

MARIA   Ooh, you sound bitter.

CASH   I drink bitter. What about you? How's your sex life?

MARIA   Perfect. I haven't got one.

CASH   Little Miss Celibate. It's a strange word. Fornicate, Masturbate, Celibate, Celibate.

MARIA   Rhymes with halibut.

CASH   (*pronouncing the last syllable as in celibate*)
              Fornicate. Masturbate, Inadequate. Don't you get
              pissed off with it?

MARIA   Not as pissed off as when I wasn't. I mean look
              how pissed off you are with this Jenny woman.

CASH   "This Jenny woman", you sound jealous.

MARIA   Jealous? Me jealous? Of some blowsy little tart,
              without half my talent or looks? Never.

CASH   It probably would have been a disaster anyway.

MARIA   Don't go with no one, go on your own. I'd love to
              do that.

CASH   Well, why don't you?

MARIA   Because I'm a woman, I can't. Now that is shit.

CASH   Why can't you?

MARIA   Because if you're a woman on your own, men see
              a sign round your neck which says "I'm a hot
              bitch, take me tonight."

CASH   Well, don't take the sign with you. You could go
              somewhere quiet, where there aren't many
              people.

MARIA   Even if you went and stayed in a clearing in the
              middle of the Brazilian rain forest a thousand
              miles from civilisation, some Indian, from some
              undiscovered tribe, would find you and waggle
              his genitals in your face.

CASH   Racist, sexist.

MARIA   Don't be glib.

CASH   Who, Maurice Glib?

MARIA   It's serious. I go into a pub on my own, I'm
           scared, so I don't go in the pub on my own. But I
           have to go to the corner shop on my own
           sometimes.

CASH   God, are you scared of going to the shop on your
           own?

MARIA   I'm scared on the streets at night. Why do you
           think you walk me home?

CASH   Well I do it on the off chance of a snog at your
           front gate. Rather fruitless campaign it is too.
           (*Senses* MARIA's *anger*.) Look it's not my fault,
           I'm on your side.

MARIA   You're a man aren't you?

CASH   Yes, but I don't approach women in the street.

MARIA   Have you ever tried to chat up a woman in a pub?

CASH   Well, yes I have, a long time ago. But that's not
           the same as attacking a woman in the street for
           Christ's sake.

MARIA   Isn't it?

CASH   Well, what about the times when I succeeded?
           When a woman agreed to go out with me after I
           met her in a pub?

MARIA   Yes, and what about the times when you didn't
           and the woman thought "God preserve me from
           half-pissed lotharios"?

CASH   I'm harmless.

MARIA   Are you?

CASH   Do you hate men?

MARIA   Only their penis.

CASH   That's quite a big bit to hate.

MARIA   It shouldn't be. It's only . . . what? A fiftieth of
            your body weight.

CASH   Half in my case. (*Leery laugh.*)

MARIA   Oh for fuck's sake.

CASH   I'm sorry.

            (*The scene changes.*)

MARIA   The annoying thing was I did feel a bit jealous.
            My sexuality was supposed to be on hold, but I
            didn't want it to disappear, I didn't want it to go
            completely unrecognised.

            (*As if the scene has ended. Then . . .*)

            I did actually weigh a bloke's penis once. Jeremy.
            Well, the bloke's name was Lenny, but I
            nicknamed his penis Jeremy. Jeremy weighed
            exactly one ounce. That was one ounce floppy.
            We never weighed it when it was erect. I don't
            think it would have been possible. A decent
            erection should defy gravity like a hot-air
            balloon. An ounce though. That's not even a
            fiftieth, is it? An ounce. That's one two-
            thousandths of the average male body. An ounce.
            That's probably less than your little finger
            weighs. At least a little finger's got a bone in it.
            If a man invested his little finger with as much
            importance as he does his willy, he'd spend his
            whole life with it up his nose. An ounce. And
            what does a vagina weigh?

            (*She gets into bed and sleeps.*)

CASH   I did actually go on holiday by myself once. I
            read eight novels, real weighty tomes — none of
            your Frederick Forsythe rubbish — real heavy
            duty Russian novels. Masterpieces. It was the
            most boring week of my life cause after you've

spent eight hours reading you just don't feel like turning in early with a good book. I kept hoping for a blistering romance with a German tourist, but the only human being I spoke to was the barman at the local taverna.

"Engleesh", he says. "Gary Lineker very good."

"Yes, yes — very good." My turn — "Nana Mouskouri, very good."

"Yes, very good. Yes, Princess Diana very nice." My turn again, and then because no other Greeks immediately sprang to mind "Socrates, very nice, very beautiful. Still very clever." Finally he topped me with, "Benny Hill very funny."

I suppose going on holiday with Maria discounts the blistering German tourist, but at least the conversation will be a little more elevated.

(MARIA *is in bed asleep.* CASH *gets into bed with her.*)

CASH   Hello Maria.

MARIA   What are you doing here?

CASH   Give us a kiss.

MARIA   I said what are you doing here?

CASH   I don't know. Really, I don't know.

(*She pulls herself up in the bed. We see she is wearing a sign saying "I'm a hot bitch, take me tonight". She takes it off and throws it away.*)

MARIA   Oh God, I'm dreaming.

CASH   Come on. All this celibacy's a load of rubbish. (*Leery.*). Give us a kiss. Come on. Half in my case. Look, it's hot, we're on holiday, we're brown.

(*Gets off of bed and sings.*)

"Moonlight becomes you it goes with your hair."
There's the foreplay, now for the action.

(*He gets back into bed.*)

CASH   Saw you on the bus. Had a good night? Can't
          have been that good, you're on your own. Pretty
          little thing like you, you shouldn't be on your
          own. How do you fancy your legs wrapped round
          my neck? You slag, you fucking slag. You cunt.

          (MARIA *screams, sits up. She sobs.* CASH
          disappears.)

          Ten years ago it was I picked up a woman in a
          pub. I was drunk but she was like DRUNK. She
          invited me back to her place for a drink and I'm
          thinking "this is amazing, I only just met her.
          What a lad I am." And we went back to this
          shitty little flat and she said be quiet, because
          there was someone asleep in another room, and I
          went to the toilet and put my contact lenses on
          two separate bits of tissue because I was
          embarrassed to take them out in front of her and
          then I lay in this strange room while she went
          and put her cap in and she came back and turned
          the light off and she wore this unfamiliar
          perfume and my bristles scratched her chin . . .
          and I could feel it, like my grandmother, and we
          giggled and sweated and thrashed around and fell
          on the floor and my dick said "No way. What are
          you doing?" And my dick got smaller and smaller
          and I tried talking dirty, and the bigger the lies,
          the more recalcitrant the dick and she, she was
          lovely. She said "Relax, it doesn't matter." But it
          did matter. There was no love, nor even any lust,
          there was only the desire to get it over with. And
          I'm thinking "Come on Dickie, this is what you
          want, you led me here." And Dick's saying "I'm
          going to sleep, I'll see you in the morning." But I
          saw it in the middle of the night as I lumbered

around and groped for the toilet and I couldn't remember where it was, or where I was and I knocked a chair over.

In the morning a little kid woke us up and said "Mummy, who's he?"

(*They are on the phone.*)

MARIA   Don't be such a snob.

CASH   But Lanzarote? You just have to say Lanzarote and people laugh. It's just a car park sticking out of the sea.

MARIA   When a man is tired of London he's tired of life, when a man is tired of Lanzarote he's been there about ten minutes. But it's either that or Tenerife.

CASH   There must be somewhere else. Something a bit more challenging. What about hang gliding down the Orinoco?

MARIA   Ok, but we'll have to get visas. We'll need to get inoculated, buy some hang gliders, and a couple of thousand pounds, learn how to hang glide . . .

CASH   Yes. It's a bit crap down the Orinoco this time of year anyway.

MARIA   Everywhere's too expensive or not hot. Why don't we compromise. We'll go to the Canaries, but pretend we've been to the Caribbean.

CASH   Or why not stay at home and invent humorous anecdotes? Who was that funny couple we met on the beach, dear?

MARIA   Oh yes them, Bob Geldof and Paula Yates.

CASH   Bob and I got on really well actually. I think Paula liked me.

MARIA   Bob fancied me. He followed us to Martinique.

CASH   But it wasn't all socialising. We did some
           watersports. We hired a dolphin for a day.

MARIA   . . . hired a dolphin for the day. Yes, I rode
           across to the coast of Venezuela.

CASH   So, Lanzarote it is then.

           (*Music.* CASH *and* MARIA *sit on "holiday" white
           chairs, at a table. They are reading a menu.*)

MARIA   It is a hole this place, isn't it? Did you ever have
           a hole? I mean did you ever dig holes as a kid?

CASH   Well, when I was in Cornwall once we had a hole
           digging competition on the beach.

MARIA   How deep was the deepest?

CASH   Oh, I don't know.

MARIA   Well, however quintessentially hole-like that hole
           was, I'm sure it couldn't compare with this hole.
           This profoundly shallow hole. It's like
           Loughborough painted white.

CASH   Let's order.

           (*They look at the menu.*)

MARIA   This isn't a menu, it's a photo album of
           cheeseburgers.

           (*An invisible waiter arrives. They both point and
           mime "this one".*)

MARIA   Y Dos Cervesas, por favor.

CASH   No, I don't want one. Un Cervesa Y un cafe con
           leche por favor. Gracias.

MARIA   I don't know why we bother to say "Cervesas"
         and "Cafe con leche". The guy knows "beer" and
         "coffee", that's his job. And . . . (*She points.*) He
         prefers it when we speak English, he can
         understand it. I'll bet he's got a 500 Peseta bet
         with the chef that I'd say "Dos Cervesas Senor"
         rather than "Oi — two beers Manuel." What a
         dump. Why do all British women on holiday look
         like Dick Emery? And all the men look like
         Lionel Blair.

CASH   I think I'll go for a walk.

MARIA   No don't. I'm sorry.

CASH   Since we've been here all you've done is drink
         and drone.

MARIA   I want you Cash. All I want is you.

CASH   You've got me. Here I am.

MARIA   Don't go.

CASH   It's not like the first time we came here, is it?

MARIA   We'd never even slept together then.

CASH   What about that romp in the garden ten years
         ago?

MARIA   Oh yes that. That wasn't even me. Well I never
         said it was — you just assumed it.

         (*They go and lie on towels facing the sea/
         audience.* MARIA *is reading.* CASH *sings the theme
         tune to "Desert Island Discs" with seagull noises
         at the end.*)

MARIA   That's a rubbish seagull. Sounds more like a
         wolf.

CASH   Here, do your ostrich for me.

(*She does.*)

That's just like the Wigan Drop. I'm a bit stoned actually.

MARIA   Are you indeed?

CASH   Yes. It was lucky bumping into that bloke on the beach — Phillipe. He works for a car hire company in the morning and sells grass on the beach in the afternoon. Ah, the tourist economy.

MARIA   You'll end up being tortured in a Spanish jail.

CASH   I hope so. How's the book? Have you got to the bit where she hacks him to death with an axe?

MARIA   What in "Pride and Prejudice"?

CASH   Oh, I thought you were reading that thriller.

MARIA   No I stopped reading that.

CASH   Why?

MARIA   I got to the bit where she hacks him to death with an axe.

CASH   How's Jane Austen?

MARIA   Don't know. I've only read five pages.

CASH   Well it's one more than you managed with Ulysses.

MARIA   You've read this haven't you?

CASH   Yes, I read it when I was fifteen. Other kids were being thrown out of pubs and necking in the park at lunchtime. I was locked away at home with Jane Austen.

MARIA   I was a necker in the park.

CASH   Were you? I wanted to be, but I couldn't get
            anyone to agree to it.

MARIA   Yes well no self-respecting fifteen year old girl
            wants to go out with a fifteen year old boy. She
            wants a mature seventeen year old with a
            motorbike and a haircut. Fifteen year old boys are
            disgusting.

CASH   I certainly was an appalling sprangle of hair and
            spots.

MARIA   Sprangle?

CASH   At the time I thought "Pride and Prejudice" was
            dead sexy. It was all foreplay, about not having
            sex, just like I wasn't. Well I was, I suppose, with
            myself. Jane Austen supplemented by the
            underwear section of the Green Shield Stamp
            catalogue. Mind you, I was so randy at the time I
            could have got a hard-on reading train
            timetables. I didn't kiss a girl till I was
            seventeen. Hilary Graves. I finally persuaded
            Hilary Graves to let me kiss her. She had a hair
            lip. It was fabulous. Who was the first boy you
            ever kissed?

MARIA   Why do you presume boy?

CASH   Oh, girl, animal, I don't know.

MARIA   He was very good looking. Looked like James
            Dean. What was his name? Michael Buckett. That
            was it. Michael Buckett.

CASH   Michael Buckett? No one's called Michael
            Buckett. Not even in plays is anyone called
            Michael Buckett.

MARIA   Well, Michael Buckett was called Michael
            Buckett.

CASH   Michael Buckett. Sounds like a refugee from a
            dirty limerick.

MARIA   He was a bit like that actually.

CASH   I wonder what ever happened to him?

MARIA   Dunno. Probably grew up to become Michael
            Skip.

CASH   A naive young farmer called Buckett,
            Once asked of a vet from Nantucket,
            What sex is this horse?
            And the vet said, of course
            I can't really tell till I fuck it.

            Are we enjoying ourselves?

MARIA   Yes.

CASH   Let's play a game.

MARIA   You and your games. What game?

CASH   I don't know, Lacrosse. Er . . . hangman. No . . .

MARIA   Have you ever played the dream game?

CASH   No.

MARIA   It's very good.

CASH   What do you do?

MARIA   I invent a dream that you've had and you have to
            guess what the dream is, by asking me questions
            to which I can answer yes or no. Is that clear?

CASH   Not really. Is this dream in colour?

MARIA   Hang on. I've got to think one up first.

MARIA   (*to audience*) I don't make anything up. All I do
            is respond to the last letter of the last word of all
            his questions. If it ends in a vowel I answer 'yes',
            if it ends in a consonant I say 'no', if it ends in a

'y' I say 'maybe'. Is that clear? It's all his own work. (*To* CASH.) Ready?

CASH   So this is my dream. Am I having sex with my dad?

MARIA   No.

CASH   Is the girl from the cheese advert in the dream?

MARIA   No.

CASH   So no sexual fantasies about cheese?

MARIA   Yes.

CASH   Do I get to shag a tub of Chambourcy?

MARIA   Maybe . . .

CASH   I'm running amok in a cheese shop?

MARIA   No, try a different tack. Where are you, for example.

CASH   I don't know, where am I?

MARIA   Yes. I can only say yes or no.

CASH   But I'm in this dream . . .

        (MARIA *goes to say 'no'.*)

CASH   Am I?

MARIA   Yes.

CASH   Am I in London?

MARIA   No.

CASH   But Britain?

MARIA   No.

CASH   Am I on earth?

MARIA   No. Very good.

CASH   I'm in space?

MARIA   Yes.

CASH   Are you there too?

MARIA   Yes.

CASH   So I'm in space with you and a lot of cheese?

MARIA   Yes.

CASH   What are we doing?

MARIA   Yes or no.

CASH   Are we nibbling Camembert and laughing?

MARIA   No.

CASH   Are we looking down on the world and laughing at the overinflated importance we give ourselves in such a vast universe?

MARIA   You are stoned, but yes.

CASH   Yes?

MARIA   No.

CASH   But do all the problems of the world look tiny?

MARIA   Maybe.

CASH   Do I get to kiss you?

MARIA   Yes.

CASH   Jesus, Maria, I'd really love to make love to you tonight. (*Beat.*) Can I?

MARIA   No.

(MARIA *continues reading her book.*)

CASH   That was the moment I went potty over her. Completely pot-pot potty. It was most unexpected, a sudden illness. I hadn't planned to ask to her bed with me, but when we got off the plane all talk of friendship and chastity fell from me like a dead skin, to reveal a glistening, carnivorous love.

MARIA   It really bloody irritated me that he assumed that when I said I was celibate it was just some device to deflect him. What really irritated me was that he was right. I had been sleeping with Andy on and off for two months.

(MARIA'S *phone rings.*)

CASH   I'll give it three more rings.

MARIA   I'll answer it after two more rings.

(*It rings four times. She picks it up.*)

CASH   Hello, Maria? It's Cash.

MARIA   Oh hi.

CASH   How are you?

MARIA   Fine.

CASH   I er, got the holiday photos back.

MARIA   Oh right. Any good?

CASH   Well the ones I took were terrible and the ones you took were terrible. So terrible it would seem

that the chemist could only bring himself to
develop one.

MARIA   What was that one of?

CASH   Well it's hard to tell because it's a bit out of
            focus and it's at a rather jaunty angle, but I think
            it's a car park. They enclosed a note to say that
            the others were even worse and that I should do
            everyone a favour and throw my camera away.

MARIA   So, terrible all round then?

CASH   Yes. Terrible. Which is how I feel.

MARIA   Yes. I got your letter.

CASH   Yes. I'm sorry.

MARIA   No you're not.

CASH   No, I'm not, I suppose. I meant it. What did you
            think of it?

MARIA   I don't know really.

CASH   Yeah, course. Funny how inarticulate one
            becomes when confronted by emotion.

MARIA   That was quite articulate.

CASH   ⎫   Yes. Look do you want . . .
MARIA   ⎭   Listen Cash, can I . . .

CASH   Sorry, go on.

MARIA   No, you say what you were going to say.

CASH   Alright. Listen do you want to see me tonight?

MARIA   Not tonight, tomorrow. What about tomorrow?

CASH   Yes, alright. Come round after work.

MARIA   Yes.

CASH   Looking forward to seeing you. I'll put some bits
            of cheese and pineapple on a stick.

MARIA   Ok.

CASH   And don't bring Michael Buckett.

MARIA   Alright.

CASH   Have you ever noticed how on TV programmes
            the characters never say goodbye at the end of a
            phone call? They just put it straight down. "See
            you Thursday" Bang. Straight down. Not where,
            or what time on Thursday.

MARIA   Yes, it's a miracle they ever meet each other.

CASH   In real phone conversation up to 75% of the call
            is spent saying goodbye.

MARIA   Yes.

CASH   So see you tomorrow then. About six thirty.

MARIA   Yes.

CASH   That's another thing — if they do say a time or a
            date on TV they never repeat it, but people
            always do.

MARIA   See you tomorrow Cash.

CASH   Yes, six thirty.

MARIA   Yes, bye.

CASH   Bye.

MARIA   Andy. Andy has got three things that interest me.
            His floppy haircut, his deeply uncomplicated
            nature and his penis. He comes in threes. He's
            got a nice bum and he's thick and he does what I

tell him. He likes hamburgers and football and
computer games. He is deeply and magnificently
predictable. To amuse myself, I took him to see
Hamlet and after fifteen minutes he leant over
and said to me, "What's the matter with him?
Why doesn't he just kill the bloke with the beard,
slap his mum, shag the bird and be done with it?"
And he's right, really. The play would be shorter,
but we'd all get to the pub quicker. He can't be
hurt, he can't hurt me. He doesn't notice, but
when I'm with him I like to wear purple nail
polish. The only odd thing about him is that he
owns a futon. I like futons, they don't give much.
I'd never want a futon though. You can't get
under a futon. Where do you go when the bomb
drops? I don't know why I didn't tell Cash about
Andy. Some unspoken contract. Maybe I should
have. Why's he gone all randy on me? Because he
thinks I've reclaimed my virginity? Can't have it.
Want it. Last night fornicating on a futon,
tonight agonizing on a sofa.

CASH   Alright, we'll make a deal. We won't talk about
              the letter for at least an hour.

MARIA   What, give you time to get pissed you mean?

CASH   "In vino veritas", there's a lot of truth in that
              phrase.

MARIA   Only if you're pissed.

CASH   Do you think you'll ever have kids?

MARIA   I don't know. Why do you ask?

CASH   It was my thirty-fifth birthday yesterday.

MARIA   No it wasn't. You were thirty-five last March.

CASH   Yes, I know, but I only kind of realised it
              yesterday. I mean some people are grandparents
              at my age.

MARIA   Oh Cash, have you gone all broody?

CASH   Well I dunno, having kids, it's like copping out.
            It's a way of fending off death. People don't have
            kids to keep the human race going, they do it as a
            long-odds bet on their own immortality. "Yes",
            they say, "I may die, it's on the cards, but surely
            my child won't, well not before me anyway, so
            I'll never know."

MARIA   Yes, it must be the saddest thing for your child to
            die before you do.

CASH   See giving birth, it's unfair on the kid. You have
            a child and he, or she, becomes the most
            important thing in your life. It becomes more
            important than you. Yeah, you have to wake up in
            the middle of the night and wipe the shit off the
            carpet and everything, but really the pressure's
            off. "You have a go," you tell the kid. "You're
            more important than I am now. I'd die for you,
            really I would, but I've tried being alive and now
            it's your turn. I'll support you and in the end I'll
            live vicariously through you, when I'm alive and
            when I'm dead." No child ever asked for that.

MARIA   Yes, but that's not it. You don't have a child as
            an intellectual exercise, you have one because you
            had sex and you had sex presumably because you
            wanted to.

CASH   Well, if it was just a question of wanting to,
            someone should have worn a condom. Preferably
            the man.

MARIA   Well maybe that's it these days, maybe that's
            love, maybe that is commitment — no condom.

CASH   I'd like not to wear a condom with you.

MARIA   Well that's alright, because you're not.

CASH   How do you know?

MARIA   An hour you said.

CASH   You don't fancy me do you?

MARIA   An hour.

CASH   I wonder if you really are celibate.

MARIA   Why do you wonder that?

CASH   I don't know, I don't think I'd fancy you if you
           really were. I mean, the sexiest thing is talking
           about sex and we've done a lot of that.

MARIA   Well you're the one who always raises it.

CASH   Yes, I know.

MARIA   An hour.

CASH   Look . . .

MARIA   An hour.

CASH   What did you have for breakfast this morning?

MARIA   Tea and toast. What did you have?

CASH   A wank over a photo of you. And a fried egg.

MARIA   Look Cash, I don't know . . .

CASH   I know you don't know, I know. That's why I
           persist. I want you to want to receive letters
           addressed to "Maria and Cash", and then "Maria
           and Cash and Gordon". At last I want to discuss
           curtains with my mother. And I want our names
           to be on the same gravestone. I want not to use a
           condom with you and I don't give up because I'm
           not convinced that you don't want these things
           too. I'm not a bad bet. I'm not skint, I'm not
           mad, I love my mother. I intend to be so loving,
           supportive and interested in you that you'll have
           to succumb. And romantic, I shall be romantic

and send you flowers and little notes I shall woo
you like you've never been wooed before. I shall
be the runaway train ran over the hill and she
blew, woo, woo. I shall probably represent the
South of England in the Woman's Own most
romantic man in Britain contest. Come on Maria,
come on Maria, here I am.

(*Pause.*)

MARIA   Gordon?

(*We hear a brief snatch of "Runaway Train".*)

MARIA   And so I am wooed. Exciting to be so desired.
Woo. Woo. Seduce, rape, charm turn on, flirt,
kiss-chase, "Georgie, Porgie pudding and pie."
To woo. So medieval. Like I'm Lady Eleanor of
Aquitaine. Whoever she is. I bet she's rich. I bet
she's got a few bob Lady Eleanor. Ellen. I do
sometimes think "Oh fuck it all, I'll marry a
millionaire, whatever he's like. I'll live in a big
house in Beverly Hills and vamp around at dinner
parties. I'll do the whole thing, I don't care,
spend the morning shopping and the afternoon in
bed with the Spanish boy who cleans the pool. I'll
have the children tanned with braces on their
teeth, the big white house, the luxury . . . the
emptiness, the divorce, the face lift, the cocaine
habit, the early death . . ." Yeah. I'm thirty-two,
how long have I got?

Cash. He woos me. He's sent me flowers nine
times. Always red roses. Red roses, that's what
pissed tourists buy in Leicester Square, isn't it? I
like the flowers actually but I'd appreciate some
freesias or a lily, and little notes . . . he wrote on
a tube ticket "I'm sorry I love you", and I only
noticed just as I was handing it to the ticket
inspector.

The really romantic things are spontaneous and
unexpected. Cash, he's too thoughtful about it.

You can't plausibly announce you're about to be romantic, you can't be analytical about it.

CASH   I think maybe I'm sending too many roses. I remember I was once having this rather one-sided affair with a woman and she was complaining that I didn't treat her well, and I sneered "Well, what do you want me to do, send you flowers?" And she said "Yes".

(CASH *is sitting on the edge of the bed, rolling a joint.* MARIA *is bending over him picking at his neck.*)

MARIA   I think this one will come out without much of a fight.

CASH   Honestly, you'd have thought at the age of thirty seven I was past the blackhead stage.

MARIA   Oh no, it's like join the dots back here.

CASH   No, no. The deal is you have to show them to me.

(*She has extracted another.*)

MARIA   Here you are.

CASH   Hmm, not bad. Bit shrivelled. Tell you what, I'll put it in the joint.

(*He drops it in joint. She continues picking.*)

CASH   They used to call me "Crater Face From the Pit" at school.

MARIA   Bit unwieldy as a nickname.

CASH   What was your nickname at school?

MARIA   Shompy.

CASH   Shompy? Why were you called that?

MARIA   I don't know.

CASH   Well you must have asked someone.

MARIA   Yes I suppose I must have but I don't remember
          their answer. Shompy.

CASH   It's funny what you can't remember.

MARIA   How do you know it's funny if you can't
          remember it?

CASH   Do you know only today someone asked me
          what's the capital of Nigeria. I couldn't
          remember. But I knew that I had known, so there
          must have been a point where the name left my
          memory.

MARIA   What are you on about?

CASH   Ow! (*She has been over-zealous with the
          blackhead removing. She stops and sits next to
          him.*) I just feel these days I'm forgetting more
          than I'm memorising. There's less and less to
          retrieve from my brain.

          (CASH *lights joint.*)

MARIA   Soon you won't be able to remember anything at
          all. It'll be rather nice like sleep.

CASH   Oh no, you remember everything when you're
          asleep.

MARIA   I don't. I'm in a black hole when I'm asleep.

CASH   Don't you dream?

MARIA   I try not to.

CASH   I dream about you often.

MARIA   I've dreamt about you.

CASH   I dreamt once we were in bed together for eight years and all we did was have sex and drink coffee.

MARIA   No you didn't.

CASH   I think I did.

(*He hands her the joint.*)

MARIA   I love you Cash, but I draw the line at smoking your blackheads.

CASH   Will you marry me?

(*Pause.*)

MARIA   You bastard. I don't know, will I?

CASH   Shall I. You should say, shall I.

MARIA   Well you make "Will you marry me" sound like "Will you be going to the hairdressers next week."

CASH   Marriage. It's an idea.

MARIA   You go out with a bloke and there are some brilliant bits. You laugh at something together, you dance, you have an orgasm, you eat chips. But they don't last long, because then there's the bits where he says something stupid, spills potato salad down his front, loses his keys, drinks too much, tells a flat joke. Marriage it seems, it seemed, was all the good bits evaporating into uncomprehending memory and all the bad bits solidifying into an eternal bore. (*Turns to* CASH.) Yes, I will, I shall marry you.

(*Music — Madame Butterfly.*)

CASH   Heart broken, three times, heart breaker maybe four times. Can't complain. A 4-3 win. When you've lost, the lowest you reach is when you phone her up to tell her exactly what she's like and how she needs to see a therapist and instead you put the phone down without saying anything. Goodbye to that.

MARIA   Three ways of knowing you've recovered from a broken heart. One, you suddenly realise you've gone a whole day without thinking of him. Two, you remember that last time you looked at your horoscope you forgot to look at his too. In a perfect world you would actually forget his name. And three, finally you fancy someone else. Goodbye to all that. Poor Andy, it turned out he could be hurt.

(*The stage is in semi-darkness. A bell tolls. A shaft of light picks out* CASH *lying on the bed.*)

CASH   (*in a voice with sickness in it — glasses? A bit hammy*) Are you all there? You were conceived on this bed, about there, you were born into this bed, and borne from it. I have spent more of my life on it than anywhere else. Its varnish has seeped into me. In this bed I have been everywhere in the world, I have made love and drunk fine wine. Sometimes lately I have urinated in it just as I did in my cot. This bed has been my life, the rest was just filling in time, now I am bedridden and this is the bed I am going out on. Your mother who shared it with me for so long gave me everything. She gave me love, hope, wisdom and she gave, oh blessed memory, the finest blow jobs. I say to you, as I said to her, never worry about a smear of marmalade on the sheets. (*Dies.*)

(*Lights up. Enter* MARIA. CASH *sits up and bounces.*)

CASH   This one's quite good.

MARIA   No, it's a horrible headboard.

CASH   What do you mean? This . . . (*Consults
              brochure.*) . . . is a 'Graduate' headboard and it's
              got "overture surround". There is a problem
              though. This bed here also has a graduate
              headboard and overture surround. But its also
              fully posturepaedic specific.

MARIA   "Posturepaedic". I remember thinking an
              orthopaedic mattress was pretty flashy.

CASH   So what I'm worried about is that this bed may
              not be fully posturepaedic specific. It doesn't say
              anything about it. It may only be slightly
              posturepaedic specific or, even worse, it may
              have no posturepaedic specifications at all.

MARIA   It's all right. Don't panic, look it's
              "Maxipaedic".

CASH   Oh, thank God.

MARIA   We've got to take this seriously.

CASH   I know, a bed is a holy shrine.

              (*A voice-over is heard: "Ladies and gentlemen
              the shop is now closing".*)

MARIA   A bed is a lot more expensive than a ring. Look
              at this one. It's got eight layers of upholstery.
              What does that mean?

CASH   Don't know. Have you noticed none of them have
              got drawers?

MARIA   Who, the shop assistants?

CASH   Oh really.

MARIA   There's a lot of them with drawers.

CASH   No, none of them are just drawers, they're easy-
              glides. I'm exhausted.

(*He lies down. Voice-over: "The shop is now closing".*)

MARIA   They'll be along to kick us out in a minute.

CASH   It says on the brochure "It's a decision you take lying down". This one's quite nice.

MARIA   (*lying down*) Why do they have to describe these beds in such stupid ways?

CASH   Sad, isn't it? But what can they say? Another flat thing with a cover. That's what beds are, always have been, always will be. Beds, they're not subject to fads. There'll never be a triangular bed.

MARIA   Yes, but I bet the bed Lazarus slept on didn't have a PS1100 spring unit. (*They giggle.*)

CASH   What about this for my last words: "Never worry about a smear of marmalade on the sheets."

MARIA   No.

CASH   Or how about "No it will be quicker if I walk across the common."

MARIA   Horrible.

          (*The lights dim.*)

CASH   They've turned the lights out!

MARIA   No one came to get us.

CASH   We are tucked away. We're on the edge of the seventh floor, it's a bit peripheral in the bed department.

MARIA   Why are we whispering?

CASH   Let's stay here.

MARIA   What?!

CASH   Stay here.

MARIA   Shall we?

CASH   It will be really exciting. The beds probably come
            alive at night.

MARIA   Maybe they dance.

CASH   Let's stay. It'll be a laugh.

MARIA   We'll get arrested in the morning.

CASH   Why? We got locked in. We should sue them. It'll
            be good publicity for them. Their bed was so
            fantastic we went to sleep while trying it out.

MARIA   We've got nothing to eat.

CASH   The food department. This is a department store,
            there's everything in the world here.

MARIA   Yes, let's move in.

CASH   You realise these beds are all virgins.

MARIA   No one's ever slept on them.

CASH   We could have it away on every bed on the store.

            (*They look round and count beds.*)

MARIA   We'll need to be here a couple of months.

            (*They turn to each other and kiss.*)

CASH   I haven't got a condom.

MARIA   Oh, what the hell.

CASH   Really?

MARIA   My period ended yesterday.

CASH   What does that mean?

               (*They start some heavy duty shagging.*)

CASH   You're very fruity tonight Miss Eastman.

MARIA   That's because I'm inclined to fuck you.

CASH   Well that's not inconvenient because I am filled
               with a throbbing desire. Do you think I should?

MARIA   I think so.

CASH   I'm planning to penetrate you in three minutes
               from now, but I shall attend to your breasts first.

               (*She turns over so she is astride him. She has her
               back to the audience. She removes her top, he
               removes his bottom — bottom bit of his pyjamas
               that is — arf, arf.*)

MARIA   Waaaah!

               (*They leap up. A shop assistant has arrived.*)

CASH   Ah, yes, we'll definitely take this one.

               (*They both light a cigarette. Next bed spins
               round on revolve. They get into it.*)

MARIA   It doesn't matter Cash. Don't worry about it.

CASH   It never happened before. Not with you.

MARIA   It doesn't matter.

CASH   Of course it matters. It's our wedding night.
               We're supposed to be going at it like the
               clappers. I should have a hard-on like a rolling
               pin.

MARIA   What with a little handle on the end?

(CASH *smiles*.)

MARIA   You are drunk.

CASH   Yes but I always am. Doesn't usually make any
          difference.

MARIA   Yes except you sometimes have to stop for a piss
          half way through. How many times have we had
          sex do you think?

CASH   You're the statistician. Two hundred, three
          hundred?

MARIA   More than that. I should think nearer five
          hundred.

CASH   They say if you put a stone in a sink every time
          you have sex in the first year of a relationship
          and then take a stone out every time after that
          there'll still be some left in the sink when you
          die.

MARIA   Well we've still got five hundred. Say we live
          another 40 years. That's about once a month for
          the rest of our lives.

CASH   Once a month. (*Pause*.) That uncle of yours . . . ?

MARIA   Which one, the drunk or the vicar?

CASH   The vicar.

MARIA   He's really pissed isn't he? Uncle Mike.

CASH   How many children has the vicar got?

MARIA   Eight.

CASH   And how many times do you think he's had sex?

MARIA   Eight. Or knowing his wife, seven.

CASH   Exactly. You just can't imagine his wrinkled old
            buttocks going up and down.

MARIA   They weren't always wrinkled.

CASH   And he's a vicar. God doesn't approve of sex
            does he? Or only to procreate.

MARIA   Only? Depends on the god. I knew a very randy
            Buddhist once.

CASH   Who was that?

MARIA   It's not such a big deal, sex, Cash. It's not only
            film stars who do it, loads of people do, even if
            it's once a month, old people, fat people, ugly
            people, sometimes the fat ones do it with the ugly
            ones, occasionally the fat old ugly one does it
            with a film star.

CASH   Everyone's a film star when they're coming.

MARIA   You are my husband.

CASH   Not yet. As it stands, or as it doesn't stand, you
            could divorce me. We haven't consummated it. I
            haven't consummated it.

MARIA   Oh God Cash, it doesn't matter.

            (*Turns to audience.*)

MARIA   Of course it matters. The first time he can't get it
            up is the night of the wedding. What does that
            mean? Like he can only do it if he's not allowed
            to. But I've learned that, you can say what you
            like to men except one thing. Never, ever even
            hint that they're no good in bed. Not even to the
            man you've just married. Especially not to the
            man you've just married.

CASH   It doesn't really matter. None of my friends had
            sex on their wedding night. All those nudge
            nudge jokes about steamy sex on the honeymoon,

they're left over from the days when couples
didn't do it before marriage. The woman was a
virgin and the man had been dutifully deflowered
by a good-hearted governess. He'd only kissed his
future wife and even that was in the company of a
blind maiden aunt. Was it ever really like that? I
asked my mother once. "Were you a virgin when
you got married?" She looked at me. "Of course I
was", she lied.

(*Turns back.*)

CASH   Tell me about the randy Buddhist.

MARIA   We used to get on the same bus.

CASH   Very erotic, public transport.

MARIA   I really fancied him.

CASH   And he chatted you up on the bus.

MARIA   No, he was too shy to chat anyone up.

CASH   So you chatted him up.

MARIA   Not in the way you're thinking.

CASH   What way was I thinking?

MARIA   Men are useless at being chatted up. You have to
make it seem like they've chatted you up.

CASH   So all my wooing was willed by you?

MARIA   (*thinks*) Maybe.

CASH   What happened to the randy Buddhist?

MARIA   Don't know. Probably grew up to become Michael
Skip. He was the "still waters are in fact a
puddle" sort.

CASH   Sod it. Let's get married.

(Blackout. Lights rise. They are in bed. She reading, him knitting.)

CASH   Who's James?

MARIA   What are you talking about?

CASH   Who's James?

MARIA   Oh don't be so stupid.

CASH   Come on, James, who is he?

MARIA   James is our son.

CASH   I know that. Not that James.

MARIA   Which James? James what?

CASH   No, James Watt invented the steam engine, some other James, James Something.

MARIA   I don't know who you're talking about. James. Well there's James Coburn the actor, James Last, the band leader. King James the First . . .

CASH   Someone called James rang up for you today. It wasn't our James because he was asleep and besides, he's incapable of speech. And I'm pretty certain it wasn't James Coburn.

MARIA   What did he say?

CASH   He said, "Hello, is Maria there?" and I said "No, shall I say who rang?" and he said, "James but not James Coburn".

MARIA   Ah well, life's not too bad, once again I haven't been rung up by James Coburn.

CASH   Why aren't you annoyed? I thought you'd say, "Why didn't you tell me before someone had rung up for me?"

MARIA   Why, why, why. You're so paranoid. You're
            suggesting that I'm not curious because I'm
            covering up for an affair that I'm having with
            someone called James.

CASH   Well are you?

MARIA   Yes. That's what you want me to say isn't it?
            Life's ok but oh no, that's no good for you. You
            need fraught. You can't just jog along happily
            and grow older.

CASH   Is that what you want? Jog along . . . oh so trite.

MARIA   Life is trite.

CASH   Even triter.

MARIA   And if it isn't trite, it's tragic. Is that what you
            want? Tragedy? Pain?

CASH   I miss intensity, we don't seem to have time to be
            intense any more. I'm half dead with habit.

MARIA   Oh poor you, at least you're not half dead with
            cancer. You want excitement why don't you join
            the Territorial Army, don't involve me.

CASH   You're bored, you're frustrated. You're having an
            affair.

MARIA   Oh for God's sake, you know I'm not. What
            possible evidence do you have that I have been
            unfaithful?

CASH   Well for one thing James, our son.

MARIA   What about him?

CASH   Why is he black?

MARIA   (pause) Why do your dreams contain so much
            dialogue? It's all talk, talk, talk.

CASH   Be fair, we are shooting through space on a
              magic carpet.

MARIA   That's true.

CASH   Look there's Cassiopeia! Hello!

MARIA   What's that?

CASH   It's a man. It's the man from the dry cleaning
              shop.

MARIA   He's on a chaise lounge.

CASH   No it's a futon.

              (CASH *zaps him dead*.)

MARIA   You've killed him, Cash.

CASH   (*shouting back*) Sorry. Ooh look at all the green
              planets. Piece of Chambourcy. Look, we're
              coming up to another galaxy.

MARIA   We ought to be getting back.

CASH   Oh God you're so sensible. Even in my dreams
              you're sensible.

MARIA   Someone's got to be.

CASH   You're the one who's seeing someone else. That's
              not very sensible.

MARIA   What do you want Cash?

CASH   I want to wake up right now.

              (*Four loud beeps of alarm. Music — Madame
              Butterfly.* CASH *starts getting books.* MARIA *exits.*)

CASH   Lagos!

(CASH *sings to the bit from Madame Butterfly that sounds like, "Ma, he's making eyes at me . . ." Lights change.*)

CASH (*to himself*) Oh God, how boring. Oh well, £15 an hour. It's only an hour. Comprehension.

(*Lays books out on table. Looks at them. Doorbell. CASH answers the door. Enter JANET — MARIA with a wig or something similar.*)

CASH Ah Janet, come in. How are you? Alright?

JANET I'm fine, Mr Cash.

CASH Did your Dad drop you off?

JANET No, I came on the bus.

CASH How's it going at school?

JANET Oh, it's boring. I bunked off again yesterday.

CASH Did you? I'm amazed you turned up to see me.

JANET Oh, I'm enjoying my private lessons with you Mr Cash.

CASH Are you indeed. Right, well I thought we'd start off with some language work. Now I'll give you two words and I want you to give me two sentences using those words which illustrate the differences between the two. Is that clear?

JANET Not really.

CASH The words are "imply" and "infer".

JANET Dunno.

CASH Now come along Janet.

JANET   When I say "I enjoy my private lessons with you, Mr Cash," I imply that I like you and you infer that I fancy you.

CASH   Very good Janet. How old are you? Seventeen? Now, let's two more words. "Disinterested" and "uninterested".

JANET   I am not UNINTERESTED in you, Mr Cash, but I hope you judge my work with DISINTEREST.

CASH   I shouldn't Janet, but I am going to kiss you.

JANET   Are you indeed.

CASH   I am going to kiss you like you've never been kissed before.

(*She screeches with laughter and returns to being* MARIA.)

CASH   Oh come on. It was going really well.

MARIA   "I am going to kiss you like you've never been kissed before." What were you going to do, kiss me with your eyebrows or something?

CASH   Oh, you've ruined it now. It was going really well. I really fancied you.

MARIA   Oh Christ, aren't I the lucky one. I have to pretend to be a seventeen year old tart before you can fancy me. It's not very flattering, Cash.

CASH   I didn't see you as tart, more sort of knowingly naive. Right, let's see your homework Janet.

MARIA   No, I'm sorry, but you've ruined it with "I am going to kiss you like you never . . ."

CASH   Alright, alright, let's do a different one.

MARIA   Yes, ok, let's do the one where you're you and I'm me and we're married like we are.

CASH	Oh no, that's boring. Come on one more, you promised.
MARIA	I don't know . . .
CASH	You'll like it when we get started, it's dead sexy. Pick a place. Where do you fancy?
MARIA	I don't know . . . Stockwell Underground station.
CASH	No, come on.
MARIA	Well you said to me once, one of your fantasies was about something about Stockwell Tube station.
CASH	Bollocks, no. Pick somewhere hot, exotic, sexy.
MARIA	Spain?
CASH	No.
MARIA	Well I don't know — Greece?
CASH	Yes, Greece, some horny little island.
MARIA	Alright, who are you?
CASH	Greece . . . a Greek fisherman, a mature fisherman with a tragic past.
MARIA	But you've come to terms with your tragedy.
CASH	Yeah, yeah. Who are you?
MARIA	Greek island. A tourist?
CASH	Yes. A German tourist.
MARIA	No, not German — Scandinavian, Danish.
CASH	Ok, Danish. Where do we meet?

MARIA   I pick you up. You're doing your nets.

CASH   What do you mean, I'm DOING my nets?

MARIA   Well that's what fishermen do isn't it? They fish
          in the morning, then in the afternoon, they faff
          around, doing their nets.

CASH   No, I want to pick you up.

MARIA   Oh alright. I'm on the beach.

CASH   What's your name?

MARIA   Find out.

          (MARIA *lies down, sunbathing.* CASH *walks up and
          down.*)

CASH   What is your name?

          (*She turns away.*)

CASH   I saw you on the beach yesterday. You are very
          beautiful girl. My name is Costas. I am
          fisherman. I have tragic past. Gary Lineker very
          good.

          (*She corpses a little bit.*)

          You like me yes? I think you are from Denmark. I
          must go, for to do my nets.

MARIA   Wait.

CASH   Yes?

MARIA   (*Danish accent*) How do you know I'm from
          Denmark?

CASH   I know many things.

MARIA   How is it you are speaking so good English?

CASH   Perhaps one day I will tell you.

MARIA   Tragic past?

            (CASH *sighs*.)

MARIA   I think you are always liking to pick up girls on
            the beach.

CASH   No, you are special girl. You are the first girl I
            have talk to since seven years.

MARIA   Go away Costas.

CASH   You want to make love with Greek man I think. I
            show you special love.

MARIA   (*English accent*) Oh fuck off Costas, you're full
            of shit.

CASH   Pretty Danish girl . . .

MARIA   No don't Cash, I don't like it.

CASH   I like you in my arms . . .

MARIA   (*shouts*) Just fuck off!

CASH   (*normal voice*) You make me feel very foolish.

MARIA   You are very foolish. I can't spend the rest of my
            life, Cash, inside your fucking head.

            (*Blackout. Music — Madame Butterfly. Lights
            rise. It is a winter night in the street. Re-enter
            CASH and MARIA some years older. They do the
            little dance of not passing properly. They finally
            succeed but CASH looks back.*)

CASH   Maria?

            (*Beat.*)

MARIA   Carl Shulman — Cash.

CASH   God, how are you?

MARIA   Fine. Fine, how are you?

CASH   Yes, great. You're looking good.

MARIA   Thanks. So how are you?

CASH   Yes, I'm fine. I heard you got married again.

MARIA   Yes, six years ago.

CASH   Was it to er . . . Martin Buckett?

MARIA   Michael Buckett. Are you married?

CASH   No.

MARIA   Kids?

CASH   Hope not. (*Pause.*) Well nice to see you.

MARIA   Yes. And you.

CASH   We're not dreaming this are we?

MARIA   I don't think so. Bye then.

          (*Out of view of each other at either side of the
          stage they both stop.* CASH *holds his head with
          hand.* MARIA *looks thoughtful.*)

CASH   Maria?

MARIA   Yes.

CASH   Does that make you Mrs Skip?

          (*She laughs.*)

          Although we knew each other so well, when she
          finally agreed to go to bed with me for the first
          time I felt like a fourteen year old with the head
          girl.

(*They are standing either side of the bed.*)

Well this is my bed.

MARIA   Yes, I thought it might be. Quite comfy.

CASH   Yes, it's an orthopaedic mattress.

MARIA   Not as hard as a futon.

CASH   Futons. I always think why pay three hundred and fifty quid for a futon, when all you've got to do is put an old duvet cover on an ironing board. Futons are incredibly uncomfortable — I expect — never actually slept on one. Have you?

MARIA   Yes.

(*She slides into it.*)

CASH   (*getting into bed*) I suppose you haven't done this for a while. Nor have I actually. (*Getting out again.*) Look, do you actually want the alarm clock on?

MARIA   No it's alright, I don't have to be up.

(CASH *gets back into bed. Pause.*)

CASH   Lights on or off? (*Gets out again.*)

MARIA   Off.

(CASH *switches the light off.*)

CASH   Well. We're in bed together then.

MARIA   Yes. Maybe we should just . . .

MARIA ⎫ . . . sleep together.
CASH ⎭ . . . sleep together.

CASH   Goodnight.

MARIA   Night.

               (*Slightly shorter pause.*)

               Doesn't creak then?

CASH   Let's find out.

MARIA   Alright.

               (*A bit of thrashing about.*)

MARIA   Cash, condom.

               (CASH *gets out of bed and turns on the light.*)

CASH   I haven't got one. Ah, the white heat at the epicentre of a love affair. The thrilling mix of love and lust, surely no feeling so intense. Maybe a gun at your head.

MARIA   Fear, doubt, relish. Relish. Chips.

CASH   I'll pick the blisters from your feet.

MARIA   Words, words, horrible words. Maybe you'll screw my sister.

CASH   Maybe you'll screw mine.

MARIA   Maybe we'll grow tired of each other.

CASH   Or you'll grow tired of me.

MARIA   Maybe I have another lover.

CASH   Have you? Who?

MARIA   I haven't any more.

CASH   Maybe I'll snore too loud.

MARIA   Maybe I'll be scared again.

CASH   Maybe there are children queuing up to be born. Maybe we shall die together.

MARIA   Maybe it wears off.

CASH   What do you want to do?

MARIA   Shall we go to bed?

(*Lights fade.* MARIA *has an orgasm — bit quicker than at the start. Set moves. Lights up.* CASH *reading paper.*)

CASH   Did you say something?

MARIA   I think we should get up.

CASH   Eh?

MARIA   I think we should get up. We've been in bed too long. I think we should get up.

(*Blackout. The end.*)